The Essential Poets

The Essential Burns

Robert Burns

BORN 25 JANUARY 1759
DIED 21 JULY 1796

The Essential
BURNS

Selected and with an
Introduction by
ROBERT CREELEY

The Ecco Press
New York

Introduction and selection copyright © 1989 by Robert Creeley
All rights reserved
Published in 1989 by The Ecco Press
26 West 17th Street, New York, N.Y. 10011
Published simultaneously in Canada by
Penguin Books Canada Ltd., Ontario
Printed in the United States of America
Design by Reg Perry
FIRST EDITION

Library of Congress Cataloging-in-Publication Data
Burns, Robert, 1759–1796.
[Poems. Selections]
The essential Burns / selected and with an introduction by Robert Creeley.
p. cm.—(The Essential poets; v. 11)
I. Creeley, Robert, 1926–   . II. Title.
III. Series: Essential poets (New York, N.Y.); v. 11.
PR4303.C74   1989   88-27277 CIP
811'.54–dc19

ISBN 0-88001-194-7 (pbk.)

Portrait of Robert Burns from the miniature by Reid
Courtesy of the Scottish National Portrait Gallery

Contents

❖

For Helen

The Essential Burns

❖

Introduction

❖❖

ROBERT BURNS is far more than an instance of singular poet, however gifted or enduring, because he shares with that select company of legend—I am thinking of Homer and Shakespeare—an accomplishment that is as much the intrinsic response of a people as it is the poet's to command it. For example, Ralph Waldo Emerson characterizes Burns aptly as "the poet of the poor, anxious, cheerful, working humanity, so had he the language of low life." Emerson sees with useful clarity the context of the power inherent, which has nothing to do with the fact or concept of "low life" but, rather, with a way of saying *things,* a cast of their argument, a tone in their expression, that will sing of itself in a music that is common indeed. So it is that Burns is able, as Emerson puts it, to transform a "*patois* unintelligible to all but natives [into] a Doric dialect of fame. It is the only example in history of a language made classic by the genius of a single man."

Expectably, the life of Robert Burns is not a simple explanation of his art, although the correspondence between the two is in this case provocative. A characteristic review of Burns' first book has the title "Surprising effects of Original Genius, exemplified in the Poetical Productions of Robert Burns, an Ayrshire Ploughman." Its author, Henry Mackenzie, is also responsible for the much echoed phrase "the Heaven-taught ploughman," which reflects the common disposition toward Burns' work. There is, of course, the question as to Burns' own intent, because he might well be presumed to have determined this *persona*—its success is immediate—in much the same way that Whitman invented his own person some fifty years later.

When *Poems, chiefly in the Scottish Dialect* was first published in 1786, Burns was twenty-seven, a small-town local, and knew that his most dependable audience would have to be finally his neighbors, if not simply himself and his friends. Even when his fame seemed secure, he was questioning and felt that Edinburgh in particular might at any moment reject him. Both poet and audience located authority in the social rather than in the classical practice of the art, such as they might presume it to be. The point is that an old time's agrarian habits and local language were fast losing place as the power of the south, the English, eroded their coherence in every way. Burns and his family were literally at the edge of this painful transformation whose effects still echo generations later in the poetry of C. M. Grieve, far better known as the embattled Scots nationalist and radical Hugh MacDiarmid.

MacDiarmid himself reflected that "T. S. Eliot was right when he said that Burns was a decadent representative of a great alien tradition, a tradition, that is to say, alien to the tradition of English letters." Such a point argues tacitly that Burns is in some way a latecomer, which, in fact, is very true, given the significant collapse of the culture that produced him. Yet his "English" poems are without exception ineffectual, much as Paul Laurence Dunbar's attempts to be "white" a century later are frustratingly disappointed. Whether Eliot had an active interest in the "great alien tradition" to which he refers is a question in itself, and MacDiarmid's repetition of the key word three times in one brief sentence is also revealing. He especially is caught in a curious classicism of intellectually proposed program, just that he *wills* the Scots language to reassert its coherence and its people also to become politically an independent and articulate collective. Paradoxically, it is Burns who most knows and is whatever "the tradition" may be said to be, because it is more than a place and time, however actual both are as obvious terms. Quite literally, it is the intense factor of human experience, of *feelings,* hot and cold, rough and smooth, pleasure and pain, *all* the particulars of language as an economy of *physical* existence, which become increasingly displaced as a demanding and abstracting "system," of whatever kind, translates their directness into a referential of generalizing orders.

The songs of Burns are most articulate as example here. Thomas Carlyle called them his "most finished, complete and truly inspired pieces. . . . The reason may be, that Song is a brief simple species of composition; and requires nothing so much for its perfection, as genuine poetic feeling, genuine music of the heart." Again MacDiarmid is useful. In 1962 he selected and wrote the introduction for a curiously genteel collection, *Burns: Love Songs* (London: Vista Books), but his sentiments are familiar enough, and his authority is to be respected:

> Although the old rural Scotland out of which these songs came has gone and can never be recovered, and its *mores* can hardly be imagined by the urbanised Scots of today, some of these songs will retain their popularity for a long time yet. Burns did a great work when he transmitted, often in refined and vastly improved form, such a great corpus of our traditional song. It was a labour of love. Too often even today Burns is thought of as a simple inspirational poet, but he worked hard and with supreme artistry on these songs, and he expressed his principle when he wrote: "I have no great faith in the boastful pretensions to intuitive propriety and unlaboured elegance. The rough material of Fine Writing is certainly the gift of Genius; but I as firmly believe that the workmanship is the united effort of Pains, Attention, and repeated Trial."

Whitman, in contrast, had trouble with both the popular estimate of Burns and the ambivalence of his own response (which had to endorse the public value while experiencing at the same time a good deal of simple competition). Thus he writes: "Finally, in any summing-up of Burns, though much is to be said in the way of fault-finding, drawing black marks, and doubtless severe literary criticism—(in the present outpouring I have 'kept myself in,' rather than allow'd any free flow)—after full retrospect of his works and life, the aforesaid 'odd-kind chiel' remains to my heart and brain as almost the tenderest, manliest, and (even if contradictory) dearest flesh-and-blood figure in all the streams and clusters of by-gone poets" ("Robert Burns as Poet and Person").

The poet who provoked this diverse response was the firstborn of William and Agnes Burnes—such was then the family spelling of their name—the former a gardener with hopes to become a nurseryman, and the latter daughter of an Ayrshire farmer named Broun. Burnes had built a two-room cottage for his wife on the seven and a half acres he rented in Alloway, and on December 15, 1757, the couple moved in. A little more than a year later Robert was born, on January 25, 1759. There were six more children, three daughters and three sons. They seem to have been a close family.

Report, however, is scant for Burns' childhood and the most impressive in its compact reference and clarity is that of Maurice Lindsay, *Robert Burns: The Man, His Work, the Legend* (1979). He speaks of the mother as hardworking, much in love with her husband, blessed with "a good singing voice, and a rich store of folk snatches." Most intriguing is the comment that "Beasts and humans shared the same roof tree, and the smokey atmosphere of the living-room must often have reeked of the pungent odours of steaming cattle." What strikes one concerning the father is his determined independence, hard indeed to maintain in the vulnerability of his employment. He had also a firm belief in the need for education, so that it was his efforts, together with the efforts of four of his neighbors (as the young schoolmaster, John Murdoch, later told it), that brought Murdoch to Alloway when Burns was going on seven.

As so often proves the case, the boy did not impress his teacher, although both he and his younger brother Gilbert were recognized as able: "They both made a rapid progress in reading and a tolerable progress in writing." Murdoch's particular memory of Robert is defensive:

> Robert's countenance was generally grave, and expressive of a serious, contemplative and thoughtful mind. Gilbert's face said, "Mirth, with thee I mean to live"; and certainly, if any person who knew the two boys, had been asked which of them was most likely to court the muses, he would surely never have guessed that Robert had a propensity of that kind.

So both brothers continued in school, despite their father's having shifted his tenancy to a seventy-acre farm east of Alloway in 1765, which proved an unwise move. The new land was poor, the terms hard to satisfy, and the family's economic situation close to foundering. By 1768 the boys were less and less frequently at Murdoch's "school," and as other patrons had moved, the teacher chose soon to leave himself. Then Burnes became his sons' schoolmaster and with some obvious effort acquired texts he thought appropriate, such as *The New Geographical, Historical and Commercial Grammar* by William Guthrie and William Derham's *Physico-Theology and Astro-Theology,* both got, so Lindsay tells us, from a "book society in Ayr."

As Robert grew older, his father depended upon him more and more for help with the farm, and this also became a limit on the boy's education. Still, it was the father's determination that his son should be taught as best he might provide, and in the summer of 1773 Burns went to Ayr for three weeks to study again with his old teacher, Murdoch, who has this recollection:

> At the end of one week I told him, that, as he was now pretty much master of the parts of [English] speech, etc., I should like

to teach him something of French pronunciation, that when he should meet with the name of a French town, ship, officer, or the like in the newspapers, he might be able to pronounce it something like a French word. Robert was glad to hear the proposal and immediately we attacked the French with great courage.

Then again, in the summer of 1776, his father sent him to a school in Kirkoswald to learn mathematics, but being seventeen, Burns expectably fell in love with a local girl. After this, as he put it, "the remaining week I staid, I did nothing but craze the faculties of my soul about her, or steal out to meet with her." The following year the family moved from the encumbrance of the farm at Mount Oliphant to Lochlie, a one-hundred-thirty-acre farm on the north bank of the Ayr in the parish of Tarbolton. So ended Burns' adolescence.

Such particulars may well seem overemphasized. Yet, as with the tale of young Lincoln's walking all that distance to return a penny or his learning to write with a piece of charcoal on the flat of a shovel, they locate a context which is definitive. Burns' education seems to have been a constant preoccupation, for him as well as for his father, and that fact belies too easy a sense of him as simply rustic. His father and his teachers had given him a far more ample base of learning than such a term could ever admit.

However, an adequate rebuttal of the myth of his sexual aggression seems much harder to accomplish, despite the evidence of the work itself. For example, the literal person speaking in Burns' poems and songs is more often a woman than is the case with any other poetry in the English language. And that voice has often a harsh reality to make clear, poignantly so, as well as to speak of the pleasures of the flesh—which, be it said, are certainly just that. Particularly the songs, which are equally Burns' authority, make all the range of shared human feeling intensely evident. Over three hundred fifty in number, these remarkable works (done first for *The Scots Musical Museum,* beginning in 1787, and then for *Select Collection of Original Scotish Airs* as well, from 1793 until Burns' death) compose an extraordinary statement of the most basic human relationships, the daily world of our familiar lives. Their one insistent fact is that *all* terms of human feeling are given clear place, and if, for example, one would read "Comin Thro' the Rye" as social introduction merely, then it must be offensive to have it revealed as sexual disposition and activity. But then as now the common world *was* common, and people were vulnerable to the common possibilities, especially paired together for the sweaty work of harvest. Such proved Burns' own coming of age, as he recalled: "In my fifteenth autumn, my Partner was a bewitching creature who just counted an Autumn less." If such comment reads now as mawkish rhetoric, the literal facts are not, and together with all the myriad details of such lives as he would finally so transform to an enduring music, they prove the ground of his work.

But James Currie's introduction to the first posthumous edition of Burns' *Works* (1800) prepares an argument that had inevitable attractions:

> The greater part of his earlier poems are written in the dialect of his country, which is obscure, if not unintelligible to Englishmen, and which though it still adheres more or less to the speech of almost every Scotsman, all the polite and ambitious are endeavouring to banish from their tongues as well as their writings. The use of it in composition naturally therefore calls up ideas of vulgarity to the mind. These singularities are encreased by the character of the poet, who delights to express himself with a simplicity that approaches to nakedness, and with an unmeasured energy that often alarms delicacy, and sometimes offends taste.

One wonders what this Liverpudlian Scots doctor would have made of the Beatles! He was not, in fact, the enemy, and his edition was for the benefit of Burns' wife and family. But in trying to accommodate his subject to the very real question of contemporary morals, this "reformed drunkard, entirely out of sympathy with the character of the man with whose poems and letters he took such astonishing, though well-meaning liberties," as Lindsay says, fixed upon Burns the label of vulgar, lustful bumpkin, faint in craft if affecting in the depiction of common feelings. So he excludes "Holy Willie's Prayer," which Sir Walter Scott was later to defend along with "The Jolly Beggars," that impressive and various cantata whose articulate common voices make clear the genius of the young poet's art.

William Burnes died in 1784, at which time Robert and Gilbert moved with the family to Mossgiel, a farm near Mauchline they had rented the year previous in order to provide themselves with a refuge from their father's possible debts. A girl who had worked in the Lochlie household, Betty Paton, became, in the following year, the mother of Burns' first child, Elizabeth, and, in some sad sense, the mother of the legend of his debauchery and callousness. Of the two poems specifically prompted by his new fatherhood, the wryly moving "A Poet's Welcome to His Love-Begotten Daughter" is convincing evidence of his affection but "The Fornicator" seems in contrast public posturing only:

> With rueful face and signs of grace
>   I pay'd the buttock-hire,
> The night was dark and thro' the park
>   I could not but convoy her . . .

The child lived with her paternal grandmother until Burns' death, at which time she returned to her own mother.

Whatever the judgment, Burns had become a poet of the first rank and the satires of this time are both shrewd and masterful. Especially effective are his attacks upon the rigid authority of the Church of Scotland, which had the power to fine and rebuke in public all whom it deemed offensive. Such poems as "Address to the Deil" not only demonstrate a control of movement and detail few indeed ever manage, but also make a most effective social ground and vocabulary for dealing with Calvinist excesses. The poet W. E. Henley (whose own "unconquerable soul" gives instance of his sympathy) called this work "the most brilliant series of assaults ever delivered against the practical bigotry of the Kirk."

With the publication of *Poems, chiefly in the Scottish Dialect* in July 1786, Burns' life divided, as it were, between the increasingly public figure of the poet and the practically invested life and survival of the literal person. His relation to Jean Armour, who bore twins to him in September of this same year, is a measure of both facts, in that her father so protested Burns' involvement with his daughter that he caused Burns to make public penance in church and threatened him with jail against his ability to post security for his immoral conduct. The immediate success of Burns' poems, however, with the income consequent, persuaded the father to drop the suit, much to Burns' relief.

Times had clearly changed for him, and with his move to Edinburgh in November 1786, no simplifying sense of innocence was longer possible. His company in Mossgiel, for example, had been for the most part middle-class tradesmen or professionals such as the lawyer Robert Aiken or Dr. Mackenzie. For a struggling young farmer these were not usual friends. In Edinburgh, with its social rank and authority, Burns found an even more various and privileged circle, and within a short time indeed he had acquired a number of patrons among the *noblesse,* as he called them, as well as a substantial cluster of the literati. It was his intent on coming to the city to undertake the printing of an expanded second edition of his *Poems,* and to this end he contacted William Creech, publisher and secretary of the Edinburgh chamber of commerce, who put him in touch with the printer William Smellie. The new edition was ready by the following April on Burns' guaranty, although Creech was much involved with the backing and distribution of the book. But he seems to have failed in responsible accounting to Burns, at least initially, although he was involved in yet another edition (1793) and also had the wry but seemingly affectionate "To William Creech" addressed to him among Burns' poems of 1787:

> *May I be Slander's common speech;*
> *A Text for Infamy to preach;*
> *And lastly, streekit out to bleach*
> > *In winter snaw*
> *When I forget thee,* WILLIE CREECH,
> > *Tho' far awa!*

The book was published with twenty-two poems added, amounting to almost a hundred more pages. One in particular, "Address to a Haggis," brought such attention to this Scottish "Heart &c. of sheep boiled in a bag with oatmeal" that it became a seasonal export, as Lindsay remarks, and is, of course, a mainstay for all the Burns Suppers held annually the world over to this day.

Through the summer and fall of 1787 Burns made "leisurely pilgrimages through Caledonia," as he wrote his friend Mrs. Dunlop, which resulted in two accounts, subsequently bowdlerized in the initial posthumous editions of the nineteenth century but eventually put right in *Robert Burns: His Associates and Contemporaries* (1943) and in a facsimile edition of the Highland tour (1927). Not long after the turn of the year Burns returned to Ayrshire and to Jean

Armour, who again bore him twins, on March 3, 1788. In April he and Armour were married, with qualifications certainly on Burns' side, but it was a deliberate commitment that lasted for the eight years left him and for the nine children thus fathered. The last, Maxwell, was being born just as Burns was buried, on July 25, 1796, and was given the name of his father's doctor and friend.

Despite his apparent fame Burns continued farming for most of these last years, beginning in 1788 at Ellisland, a farm leased from a would-be patron, Patrick Miller, who described it as being in "the most miserable state of exhaustion, and all the tenants in poverty," at the time of his purchase. Burns had, in fact, to build a house for himself and his family before he could properly move in. At the same time he had just completed his initial training for the excise, a method of taxing goods of a wide variety at the place of their manufacture, which procedure required a staggering knowledge of all the varying rates that might exist for even different grades of one article. But Burns was grateful for the resource it gave him for income apart from farming, and although he had often to ride as many as two hundred miles a week, and to see to the horse's welfare in addition to keeping his accounts in good order, it was a pay that was higher than the average schoolmaster's, minister's, or farmer's, and so he much valued it.

It is remarkable that he managed such labors and kept up as well a steady production of songs for James Johnson's *The Scots Musical Museum* and, as earlier remarked, in 1792 and continuing, for George Thomson's *Select Collection of Original Scotish Airs* also. In 1793 the family moved to Mill Vennel, Dumfries, where Burns kept his work as an exciseman at the Dumfries port division. It was the most substantial city, albeit small, in which he was to live for any length of time, and it proved a place of active friends as always. One, Robert Syme, gives this sense of him:

The poet's expression varied perpetually, according to the idea that predominated in his mind; and it was beautiful to remark how well the play of lips indicated the sentiment he was about to utter. His eyes and lips—the first remarkable for fire, and the second for flexibility—formed at all times an index to his mind.

But the times and his own habits made no simple accommodation ever. Just in his mid-thirties, finally in some small respect secure in his employment—though he had also just weathered a charge of malfeasance, the result of his possession and/or purchase of firearms gotten from a smuggler's vessel, which he then sent to the French Convention as instance of his sympathy—and confident in respect and, at least generally, in situation, he became significantly ill. It was at this time also that his behavior caused a break in his friendship with Mrs. Walter Riddell, the last of his significant women friends and possibly the most brilliant. His relation with her was not simply resolved by his usual habits with "the sex," as he called women. But characteristic drinking and determinations of an awkwardly romantic kind had caused her sister-in-law, Mrs. Robert Riddell, intense, public embarrassment, and Burns' wry and insistent repentance—"I daresay this is the first epistle you ever received from this nether world. I write you from the regions of Hell, amid the horrors of the damned"—might entertain this relative privately, but it was no solution for Maria Riddell's own very public dilemma.

So too his anti-Royalist feelings and England's war with France made the time more generally a hard one, despite warm and specific friends, and the local famine in Dumfries brought it all home. Nonetheless, in 1795 Burns helped organize the Dumfries Volunteers in support of the Crown. But a song he wrote in their name makes clear his dilemma and ends with this verse:

> The wretch that would a *Tyrant* own,
>   And the wretch, his true-sworn brother,
> Who'd set the *Mob* above the *Throne*,
>   May they be damn'd together!
> Who will not sing, *God Save the King*,
>   Shall hang as high's the steeple;
> But while we sing, *God Save the King*,
>   We'll ne'er forget *The People*!

Not long afterward, Burns suffered the first of the decisive attacks that he thought to be rheumatic fever but which were, one can now believe, more probably effects of the straining of his heart from hard work as a boy. Lindsay recounts the "barbarous treatment" he then underwent, at a reputed "spa" some nine miles southeast of Dumfries: "Every day he waded far out over the shallow Solway sands until he stood armpit-high in the cold sea-water." One recalls Lawrence's futile attempts to survive tuberculosis by brutal daily walks he had thought might help him. Our common humanity has only its own small people for company at last.

Before I thought to undertake this selection of Robert Burns' undying work, I knew all too little of him, although his poems and songs were truly among my first delights in hearing and reading poetry as a boy. He defined a care, a manliness, and a perceiving humor for me that I've never forgotten. My sister, Helen, had visited the very house he was born in, and when I told her the little I'd finally discovered, she still knew far better than I just where the cows must have been and where the children. But one *can* learn—and here it is the greatest art that can so sing, and the greatest heart that sustained it.

Finally, acknowledgments and thanks are due to all of Burns' editors and biographers, even the obtuse Dr. Currie, because I have made clear my own favorite but realize that no one story is the end of anything. There are the two standard editions of Burns' poems easily available: James Kinsley's edition of *Poems and Songs* (Oxford: Oxford University Press, 1968) and Raymond Bentman's edition (based on W. E. Henley and Thomas F. Henderson's *The Centenary Burns,* London, 1896–1897), *The Poetical Works of Burns* (Boston: Houghton Mifflin, 1974). But one will hear Burns everywhere and forever—till old acquaintance be forgot.

—ROBERT CREELEY

Poems

FROM *POEMS, CHIEFLY IN THE SCOTTISH DIALECT*

Address to the Deil

O Prince! O Chief of many thronèd pow'rs!
That led th' embattl'd seraphim to war.
—MILTON

I

O thou! whatever title suit thee—
Auld Hornie, Satan, Nick, or Clootie—
Wha in yon cavern grim an' sootie,
           Clos'd under hatches,
Spairges about the brunstane cootie,
           To scaud poor wretches!

II

Hear me, Auld Hangie, for a wee,
An' let poor damnèd bodies be;
I'm sure sma' pleasure it can gie,
           Ev'n to a deil,
To skelp an' scaud poor dogs like me
           An' hear us squeel.

III

Great is thy pow'r an' great thy fame;
Far kend an' noted is thy name;
An' tho' yon lowin heugh 's thy hame,
           Thou travels far;
An' faith! thou 's neither lag, nor lame,
              Nor blate, nor scaur.

IV

Whyles, ranging like a roarin lion,
For prey, a' holes an' corners trying;
Whyles, on the strong-wing'd tempest flyin,
           Tirlin the kirks;
Whyles, in the human bosom pryin,
              Unseen thou lurks.

V

I 've heard my rev'rend graunie say,
In lanely glens ye like to stray;
Or, where auld ruin'd castles grey
           Nod to the moon,
Ye fright the nightly wand'rer's way
              Wi' eldritch croon.

VI

When twilight did my graunie summon,
To say her pray'rs, douce, honest woman!
Aft yont the dyke she 's heard you bummin,
           Wi' eerie drone;
Or, rustlin, thro' the boortrees comin,
              Wi' heavy groan.

VII

Ae dreary, windy, winter night,
The star shot down wi' sklentin light,
Wi' you mysel, I gat a fright:
        Ayont the lough,
Ye, like a rash-buss, stood in sight,
        Wi' waving sugh.

VIII

The cudgel in my nieve did shake,
Each bristl'd hair stood like a stake;
When wi' an eldritch, stoor "quaick, quaick,"
        Amang the springs,
Awa ye squatter'd like a drake,
        On whistling wings.

IX

Let warlocks grim, an' wither'd hags,
Tell how wi' you, on ragweed nags,
They skim the muirs an' dizzy crags,
        Wi' wicked speed;
And in kirk-yards renew their leagues,
        Owre howkit dead.

X

Thence, countra wives, wi' toil an' pain,
May plunge an' plunge the kirn in vain;
For O! the yellow treasure's taen
        By witching skill;
An' dawtit, twal-pint hawkie's gaen
        As yell's the bill.

XI

Thence, mystic knots mak great abuse
On young guidmen, fond, keen an' croose;
When the best wark-lume i' the house,
   By cantraip wit,
Is instant made no worth a louse,
   Just at the bit.

XII

When thowes dissolve the snawy hoord,
An' float the jinglin icy boord,
Then, water-kelpies haunt the foord,
   By your direction,
An' nighted trav'llers are allur'd
   To their destruction.

XIII

And aft your moss-traversing spunkies
Decoy the wight that late an' drunk is:
The bleezin, curst, mischievous monkies
   Delude his eyes,
Till in some miry slough he sunk is,
   Ne'er mair to rise.

XIV

When Masons' mystic word an' grip
In storms an' tempests raise you up,
Some cock or cat your rage maun stop,
   Or, strange to tell!
The youngest brother ye wad whip
   Aff straught to hell.

XV

Lang syne in Eden's bonie yard,
When youthfu' lovers first were pair'd,
An' all the soul of love they shar'd,
        The raptur'd hour,
Sweet on the fragrant flow'ry swaird,
        In shady bow'r:

XVI

Then you, ye auld, snick-drawing dog!
Ye cam to Paradise incog,
An' play'd on man a cursed brogue
        (Black be your fa'!),
An' gied the infant warld a shog,
        'Maist ruin'd a'.

XVII

D' ye mind that day when in a bizz
Wi' reekit duds, an' reestit gizz,
Ye did present your smoutie phiz
        'Mang better folk;
An' sklented on the man of Uzz
        Your spitefu' joke?

XVIII

An' how ye gat him i' your thrall,
An' brak him out o' house an' hal',
While scabs an' botches did him gall,
        Wi' bitter claw;
An' lows'd his ill-tongu'd wicked scaul—
        Was warst ava?

XIX

But a' your doings to rehearse,
Your wily snares an' fechtin fierce,
Sin' that day Michael did you pierce
                    Down to this time,
Wad ding a Lallan tongue, or Erse,
                    In prose or rhyme.

XX

An' now, Auld Cloots, I ken ye're thinkin,
A certain Bardie's rantin, drinkin,
Some luckless hour will send him linkin,
                    To your black Pit;
But, faith! he'll turn a corner jinkin,
                    An' cheat you yet.

XXI

But fare-you-weel, Auld Nickie-Ben!
O, wad ye tak a thought an' men'!
Ye aiblins might—I dinna ken—
                    Still hae a stake:
I'm wae to think upo' yon den,
                    Ev'n for your sake!

A Dream

Thoughts, words, and deeds, the Statute blames with reason;
But surely *Dreams* were ne'er indicted Treason.

I

Guid-mornin to your Majesty!
    May Heaven augment your blisses,

On ev'ry new birth-day ye see,
  A humble Poet wishes!
My Bardship here, at your Levee,
    On sic a day as this is,
Is sure an uncouth sight to see,
    Amang thae birth-day dresses
                Sae fine this day.

II

I see ye 're complimented thrang,
    By monie a lord an' lady;
God Save the King 's a cuckoo sang
    That 's unco easy said ay:
The poets, too, a venal gang,
    Wi' rhymes weel-turn'd an' ready,
Wad gar you trow ye ne'er do wrang,
    But ay unerring steady,
                On sic a day.

III

For me! before a Monarch's face,
    Ev'n there I winna flatter;
For neither pension, post, nor place,
    Am I your humble debtor:
So, nae reflection on your Grace,
    Your Kingship to bespatter;
There 's monie waur been o' the race,
    And aiblins ane been better
                Than you this day.

IV

'T is very true my sovereign King,
    My skill may weel be doubted;

But facts are chiels that winna ding,
   And downa be disputed:
Your royal nest, beneath your wing,
   Is e'en right reft and clouted,
And now the third part o' the string,
   An' less, will gang about it
               Than did ae day.

V

Far be 't frae me that I aspire
   To blame your legislation,
Or say, ye wisdom want, or fire
   To rule this mighty nation:
But faith! I muckle doubt, my sire,
   Ye've trusted ministration
To chaps wha in a barn or byre
   Wad better fill'd their station,
               Than courts yon day.

VI

And now ye've gien auld Britain peace,
   Her broken shins to plaister;
Your sair taxation does her fleece,
   Till she has scarce a tester:
For me, thank God, my life's a lease,
   Nae bargain wearin faster,
Or faith! I fear, that wi' the geese,
   I shortly boost to pasture
               I' the craft some day.

VII

I'm no mistrusting Willie Pitt,
   When taxes he enlarges,

(An' Will's a true guid fallow's get,
  A name not envy spairges),
That he intends to pay your debt,
  An' lessen a' your charges;
But, God sake! let nae saving fit
  Abridge your bonie barges
              An' boats this day.

VIII

Adieu, my Liege! may Freedom geck
  Beneath your high protection;
An' may ye rax Corruption's neck,
  And gie her for dissection!
But since I'm here I'll no neglect,
  In loyal, true affection,
To pay your Queen, wi' due respect,
  My fealty an' subjection
              This great birth-day.

IX

Hail, Majesty most Excellent!
  While nobles strive to please ye,
Will ye accept a compliment,
  A simple Bardie gies ye?
Thae bonie bairntime Heav'n has lent,
  Still higher may they heeze ye
In bliss, till Fate some day is sent,
  For ever to release ye
              Frae care that day.

X

For you, young Potentate o' Wales,
  I tell your Highness fairly,

Down Pleasure's stream, wi' swelling sails,
    I'm tauld ye're driving rarely;
But some day ye may gnaw your nails,
    An' curse your folly sairly,
That e'er ye brak Diana's pales,
    Or rattl'd dice wi' Charlie
                By night or day.

XI

Yet aft a ragged cowte's been known,
    To mak a noble aiver;
So, ye may doucely fill a throne,
    For a' their clish-ma-claver:
There, him at Agincourt wha shone,
    Few better were or braver;
And yet, wi' funny, queer Sir John,
    He was an unco shaver
                For monie a day.

XII

For you, right rev'rend Osnaburg,
    Nane sets the lawn-sleeve sweeter,
Altho' a ribban at your lug
    Wad been a dress completer:
As ye disown yon paughty dog,
    That bears the keys of Peter,
Then swith! an' get a wife to hug,
    Or trowth, ye'll stain the mitre
                Some luckless day!

XIII

Young, royal Tarry-breeks, I learn,
    Ye've lately come athwart her—

A glorious galley, stem an' stern
   Weel rigg'd for Venus' barter;
But first hang out that she 'll discern
   Your hymeneal charter;
Then heave aboard your grapple-airn,
   An', large upon her quarter,
               Come full that day.

XIV

Ye, lastly, bonie blossoms a',
   Ye royal lasses dainty,
Heav'n mak you guid as weel as braw,
   An' gie you lads a-plenty!
But sneer na British boys awa!
   For kings are unco scant ay,
An' German gentles are but sma':
   They 're better just than want ay
               On onie day.

XV

God bless you a'! consider now,
   Ye 're unco muckle dautet;
But ere the course o' life be through,
   It may be bitter sautet:
An' I hae seen their coggie fou,
   That yet hae tarrow't at it;
But or the day was done, I trow,
   The laggen they hae clautet
               Fu' clean that day.

To a Mouse

ON TURNING HER UP IN HER NEST
WITH THE PLOUGH, NOVEMBER, 1785

I

Wee, sleekit, cowrin, tim'rous beastie,
O, what a panic's in thy breastie!
Thou need na start awa sae hasty
             Wi' bickering brattle!
I wad be laith to rin an' chase thee,
             Wi' murdering pattle!

II

I'm truly sorry man's dominion
Has broken Nature's social union,
An' justifies that ill opinion
             Which makes thee startle
At me, thy poor, earth-born companion
             An' fellow mortal!

III

I doubt na, whyles, but thou may thieve;
What then? poor beastie, thou maun live
A daimen icker in a thrave
             'S a sma' request;
I'll get a blessin wi' the lave,
             An' never miss 't!

IV

Thy wee-bit housie, too, in ruin!
Its silly wa's the win's are strewin!
An' naething, now, to big a new ane,
             O' foggage green!

An' bleak December's win's ensuin,
                    Baith snell an' keen!

V

Thou saw the fields laid bare an' waste,
An' weary winter comin fast,
An' cozie here, beneath the blast,
                    Thou thought to dwell,
Till crash! the cruel coulter past
                    Out thro' thy cell.

VI

That wee bit heap o' leaves an' stibble,
Has cost thee monie a weary nibble!
Now thou's turned out, for a' thy trouble,
                    But house or hald,
To thole the winter's sleety dribble,
                    An' cranreuch cauld!

VII

But Mousie, thou art no thy lane,
In proving foresight may be vain:
The best-laid schemes o' mice an' men
                    Gang aft agley,
An' lea'e us nought but grief an' pain,
                    For promis'd joy!

VIII

Still thou art blest, compared wi' me!
The present only toucheth thee:
But och! I backward cast my e'e,
                    On prospects drear!
An' forward, tho' I canna see,
                    I guess an' fear!

Epistle to Davie, a Brother Poet

JANUARY

I

While winds frae aff Ben-Lomond blaw,
And bar the doors wi' drivin' snaw,
   And hing us owre the ingle,
I set me down to pass the time,
And spin a verse or twa o' rhyme,
   In hamely, westlin jingle:
While frosty winds blaw in the drift,
   Ben to the chimla lug,
I grudge a wee the great-folk's gift,
   That live sae bien an' snug:
      I tent less, and want less
         Their roomy fire-side;
      But hanker, and canker,
         To see their cursèd pride.

II

It 's hardly in a body's pow'r,
To keep, at times, frae being sour,
   To see how things are shar'd;
How best o' chiels are whyles in want,
While coofs on countless thousands rant,
   And ken na how to ware 't;
But Davie, lad, ne'er fash your head,
   Tho' we hae little gear;
We're fit to win our daily bread,
   As lang 's we 're hale and fier:
      "Mair spier na, nor fear na,"
         Auld age ne'er mind a feg;

The last o't, the warst o't,
   Is only but to beg.

III

To lie in kilns and barns at e'en,
When banes are craz'd, and bluid is thin,
   Is, doubtless, great distress!
Yet then content could make us blest;
Ev'n then, sometimes, we'd snatch a taste
   Of truest happiness.
The honest heart that's free frae a'
   Intended fraud or guile,
However Fortune kick the ba',
   Has ay some cause to smile;
      And mind still, you'll find still,
         A comfort this nae sma';
      Nae mair then, we'll care then,
         Nae farther can we fa'.

IV

What tho', like commoners of air,
We wander out, we know not where,
   But either house or hal'?
Yet Nature's charms, the hills and woods,
The sweeping vales, and foaming floods,
   Are free alike to all.
In days when daisies deck the ground,
   And blackbirds whistle clear,
With honest joy our hearts will bound,
   To see the coming year:
      On braes when we please then,
         We'll sit an' sowth a tune;
      Syne rhyme till't we'll time till't,
         An' sing't when we hae done.

V

It's no in titles nor in rank:
It's no in wealth like Lon'on Bank,
   To purchase peace and rest.
It's no in makin muckle, mair;
It's no in books, it's no in lear,
   To make us truly blest:
If happiness hae not her seat
   An' centre in the breast,
We may be wise, or rich, or great,
   But never can be blest!
      Nae treasures nor pleasures
         Could make us happy lang;
      The heart ay's the part ay
         That makes us right or wrang.

VI

Think ye, that sic as you and I,
Wha drudge and drive thro' wet and dry,
   Wi' never ceasing toil;
Think ye, are we less blest than they,
Wha scarcely tent us in their way,
   As hardly worth their while?
Alas! how oft, in haughty mood,
   God's creatures they oppress!
Or else, neglecting a' that's guid,
   They riot in excess!
      Baith careless and fearless
         Of either Heaven or Hell;
      Esteeming and deeming
         It a' an idle tale!

VII

Then let us chearfu' acquiesce,
Nor make our scanty pleasures less
    By pining at our state:
And, even should misfortunes come,
I here wha sit hae met wi' some,
    An's thankfu' for them yet,
They gie the wit of age to youth;
    They let us ken oursel;
They make us see the naked truth,
    The real guid and ill:
        Tho' losses and crosses
            Be lessons right severe,
        There's wit there, ye'll get there,
            Ye'll find nae other where.

VIII

But tent me, Davie, ace o' hearts!
(To say aught less wad wrang the cartes,
    And flatt'ry I detest)
This life has joys for you and I;
And joys that riches ne'er could buy,
    And joys the very best.
There's a' the pleasures o' the heart,
    The lover an' the frien':
Ye hae your Meg, your dearest part,
    And I my darling Jean!
        It warms me, it charms me
            To mention but her name:
        It heats me, it beets me,
            And sets me a' on flame!

IX

O all ye Pow'rs who rule above!
O Thou whose very self art love!
   Thou know'st my words sincere!
The life-blood streaming thro' my heart,
Or my more dear immortal part,
   Is not more fondly dear!
When heart-corroding care and grief
   Deprive my soul of rest,
Her dear idea brings relief
   And solace to my breast,
     Thou Being All-seeing,
      O, hear my fervent pray'r!
     Still take her, and make her
      Thy most peculiar care!

X

All hail! ye tender feelings dear!
The smile of love, the friendly tear,
   The sympathetic glow!
Long since, this world's thorny ways
Had number'd out my weary days,
   Had it not been for you!
Fate still has blest me with a friend
   In every care and ill;
And oft a more endearing band,
   A tie more tender still.
     It lightens, it brightens
      The tenebrific scene,
     To meet with, and greet with
      My Davie or my Jean!

XI

O, how that Name inspires my style!
The words come skelpin' rank an' file,
   Amaist before I ken!
The ready measure rins as fine,
As Phœbus and the famous Nine
   Were glowrin owre my pen.
My spaviet Pegasus will limp,
   Till ance he's fairly het;
And then he 'll hilch, an' stilt, an' jimp,
   And rin an unco fit;
      But least then, the beast then
        Should rue this hasty ride,
      I 'll light now, and dight now
        His sweaty, wizen'd hide.

To a Louse

ON SEEING ONE ON A LADY'S BONNET AT CHURCH

I

Ha! whare ye gaun, ye crowlin ferlie?
Your impudence protects you sairly,
I canna say but ye strunt rarely
         Owre gauze and lace,
Tho' faith! I fear ye dine but sparely
         On sic a place.

II

Ye ugly, creepin, blastit wonner,
Detested, shunn'd by saunt an' sinner,
How daur ye set your fit upon her—
         Sae fine a lady!

Gae somewhere else and seek your dinner
            On some poor body.

III

Swith! in some beggar's hauffet squattle:
There ye may creep, and sprawl, and sprattle,
Wi' ither kindred, jumping cattle,
            In shoals and nations;
Whare horn nor bane ne'er daur unsettle
            Your thick plantations.

IV

Now haud you there! ye 're out o' sight,
Below the fatt'rils, snug an' tight;
Na, faith ye yet! ye 'll no be right,
            Till ye 've got on it—
The vera tapmost, tow'ring height
            O' Miss's bonnet.

V

My sooth! right bauld ye set your nose out,
As plump an' grey as onie grozet:
O for some rank, mercurial rozet,
            Or fell, red smeddum,
I 'd gie ye sic a hearty dose o 't,
            Wad dress your droddum.

VI

I wad na been surpris'd to spy
You on an auld wife's flainen toy;
Or aiblins some bit duddie boy,
            On 's wyliecoat;
But Miss's fine Lunardi! fye!
            How daur ye do 't?

VII

O Jenny, dinna toss your head,
An' set your beauties a' abread!
Ye little ken what cursèd speed
                    The blastie's makin!
Thae winks an' finger-ends, I dread,
                    Are notice takin!

VIII

O wad some Power the giftie gie us
To see oursels as ithers see us!
It wad frae monie a blunder free us,
                    An' foolish notion:
What airs in dress an' gait wad lea'e us,
                    An' ev'n devotion!

Epistle to J. Lapraik

AN OLD SCOTTISH BARD, APRIL 1, 1785

I

While briers an' woodbines budding green,
And paitricks scraichin loud at e'en,
An' morning poussie whiddin seen,
                    Inspire my Muse,
This freedom, in an unknown frien'
                    I pray excuse.

II

On Fasten-e'en we had a rockin,
To ca' the crack and weave our stockin;
And there was muckle fun and jokin,
                    Ye need na doubt;

At length we had a hearty yokin,
                    At "sang about."

III

There was ae sang, among the rest,
Aboon them a' it pleas'd me best,
That some kind husband had addrest
                    To some sweet wife:
It thirl'd the heart-strings thro' the breast,
                    A' to the life.

IV

I've scarce heard ought describ'd sae weel,
What gen'rous, manly bosoms feel;
Thought I, "Can this be Pope or Steele,
                    Or Beattie's wark?"
They tald me 't was an odd kind chiel
                    About Muirkirk.

V

It pat me fidgin-fain to hear 't,
An' sae about him there I spier't;
Then a' that kent him round declar'd
                    He had ingine;
That nane excell'd it, few cam near 't,
                    It was sae fine:

VI

That, set him to a pint of ale,
An' either douce or merry tale,
Or rhymes an' sangs he 'd made himsel,
                    Or witty catches,
'Tween Inverness an' Teviotdale,
                    He had few matches.

VII

Then up I gat, an' swoor an aith,
Tho' I should pawn my pleugh an' graith,
Or die a cadger pownie's death,
           At some dyke-back,
A pint an' gill I'd gie them baith,
           To hear your crack.

VIII

But, first an' foremost, I should tell,
Amaist as soon as I could spell,
I to the crambo-jingle fell;
           Tho' rude an' rough—
Yet crooning to a body's sel,
           Does weel eneugh.

IX

I am nae poet, in a sense;
But just a rhymer like by chance,
An' hae to learning nae pretence;
           Yet, what the matter?
Whene'er my Muse does on me glance,
           I jingle at her.

X

Your critic-folk may cock their nose,
And say, "How can you e'er propose,
You wha ken hardly verse frae prose,
           To mak a sang?"
But, by your leaves, my learned foes,
           Ye're maybe wrang.

XI

What's a' your jargon o' your Schools,
Your Latin names for horns an' stools?
If honest Nature made you fools,
                              What sairs your grammers?
Ye'd better taen up spades and shools,
                              Or knappin-hammers.

XII

A set o' dull, conceited hashes
Confuse their brains in college-classes,
They gang in stirks, and come out asses,
                              Plain truth to speak;
An' syne they think to climb Parnassus
                              By dint o' Greek!

XIII

Gie me ae spark o' Nature's fire,
That's a' the learning I desire;
Then, tho' I drudge thro' dub an' mire
                              At pleugh or cart,
My Muse, tho' hamely in attire,
                              May touch the heart.

XIV

O for a spunk o' Allan's glee,
Or Fergusson's, the bauld an' slee,
Or bright Lapraik's, my friend to be,
                              If I can hit it!
That would be lear eneugh for me,
                              If I could get it.

XV

Now, sir, if ye hae friends enow,
Tho' real friends I b'lieve are few;
Yet, if your catalogue be fow,
            I 'se no insist:
But, gif ye want ae friend that 's true,
            I'm on your list.

XVI

I winna blaw about mysel,
As ill I like my fauts to tell;
But friends, an' folks that wish me well,
            They sometimes roose me;
Tho', I maun own, as monie still
            As far abuse me.

XVII

There 's ae wee faut they whyles lay to me,
I like the lasses—Gude forgie me!
For monie a plack they wheedle frae me
            At dance or fair;
Maybe some ither thing they gie me,
            They weel can spare.

XVIII

But Mauchline Race or Mauchline Fair,
I should be proud to meet you there:
We 'se gie ae night's discharge to care,
            If we forgather;
And hae a swap o' rhymin-ware
            Wi' ane anither.

XIX

The four-gill chap, we 'se gar him clatter,
An' kirsen him wi' reekin water;
Syne we 'll sit down an' tak our whitter,
        To cheer our heart;
An' faith, we 'se be acquainted better
        Before we part.

XX

Awa ye selfish, warly race,
Wha think that havins, sense, an' grace,
Ev'n love an' friendship should give place
        To Catch-the-Plack!
I dinna like to see your face,
        Nor hear your crack.

XXI

But ye whom social pleasure charms,
Whose hearts the tide of kindness warms,
Who hold your being on the terms,
        "Each aid the others,"
Come to my bowl, come to my arms,
        My friends, my brothers!

XXII

But, to conclude my lang epistle,
As my auld pen 's worn to the grissle,
Twa lines frae you wad gar me fissle,
        Who am most fervent,
While I can either sing or whistle,
        Your friend and servant.

FROM THE EDINBURGH EDITION,
1787

Death and Doctor Hornbook

A TRUE STORY

I

Some books are lies frae end to end,
And some great lies were never penn'd:
Ev'n ministers, they hae been kend,
    In holy rapture,
A rousing whid at times to vend,
     And nail't wi' Scripture.

II

But this that I am gaun to tell,
Which lately on a night befel,
Is just as true's the Deil's in hell
    Or Dublin city:
That e'er he nearer comes oursel
     'S a muckle pity!

III

The clachan yill had made me canty,
I was na fou, but just had plenty:
I stacher'd whyles, but yet took tent ay
    To free the ditches;
An' hillocks, stanes, an' bushes, kend ay
     Frae ghaists an' witches.

IV

The rising moon began to glowr
The distant Cumnock Hills out-owre:
To count her horns, wi' a' my pow'r
   I set mysel;
But whether she had three or four,
   I cou'd na tell.

V

I was come round about the hill,
And todlin down on Willie's mill,
Setting my staff wi' a' my skill
   To keep me sicker;
Tho' leeward whyles, against my will,
   I took a bicker.

VI

I there wi' *Something* does forgather,
That pat me in an eerie swither;
Au awfu' scythe, out-owre ae shouther,
   Clear-dangling, hang;
A three-tae'd leister on the ither
   Lay, large an' lang.

VII

Its stature seem'd lang Scotch ells twa;
The queerest shape that e'er I saw,
For fient a wame it had ava;
   And then its shanks,
They were as thin, as sharp an' sma'
   As cheeks o' branks.

VIII

"Guid-een," quo' I; "Friend! hae ye been mawin,
When ither folk are busy sawin?"
It seem'd to mak a kind o' stan',
　　　　But naething spak.
At length, says I: "Friend! whare ye gaun?
　　　　Will ye go back?"

IX

It spak right howe: "My name is Death,
But be na' fley'd." Quoth I: "Guid faith,
Ye're may be come to stap my breath;
　　　　But tent me, billie:
I red ye weel, take care o' skaith,
　　　　See, there's a gully!"

X

"Gudeman," quo' he, "put up your whittle,
I'm no design'd to try its mettle;
But if I did, I wad be kittle
　　　　To be mislear'd:
I wad na mind it, no that spittle
　　　　Out-owre my beard."

XI

"Weel, weel!" says I, "a bargain be't;
Come, gie's your hand, an' say we're gree't;
We'll ease our shanks, an' tak a seat:
　　　　Come, gie's your news:
This while ye hae been monie a gate,
　　　　At monie a house."

XII

"Ay, ay!" quo' he, an' shook his head,
"It 's e'en a lang, lang time indeed
Sin' I began to nick the thread
              An' choke the breath:
Folk maun do something for their bread,
              An' sae maun Death.

XIII

"Sax thousand years are near-hand fled
Sin' I was to the butching bred,
An' monie a scheme in vain 's been laid
              To stap or scar me;
Till ane Hornbook 's ta'en up the trade,
              And faith! he'll waur me.

XIV

"Ye ken Jock Hornbook i' the clachan?
Deil mak his king's-hood in a spleuchan!—
He 's grown sae weel acquaint wi' *Buchan*
              And ither chaps,
The weans haud out their fingers laughin,
              An' pouk my hips.

XV

"See, here 's a scythe, an' there 's a dart,
They hae pierc'd monie a gallant heart;
But Doctor Hornbook wi' his art
              An' cursed skill,
Has made them baith no worth a fart,
              Damn'd haet they 'll kill!

XVI

" 'T was but yestreen, nae farther gane,
I threw a noble throw at ane;
Wi' less, I 'm sure, I 've hundreds slain;
            But Deil-ma-care!
It just played dirl on the bane,
            But did nae mair.

XVII

"Hornbook was by wi' ready art,
An' had sae fortify'd the part,
That when I lookèd to my dart,
            It was sae blunt,
Fient haet o 't wad hae pierc'd the heart
            Of a kail-runt.

XVIII

"I drew my scythe in sic a fury,
I near-hand cowpit wi' my hurry,
But yet the bauld Apothecary
            Withstood the shock:
I might as weel hae try'd a quarry
            O' hard whin-rock.

XIX

"Ev'n them he canna get attended,
Altho' their face he ne'er had kend it,
Just shit in a kail-blade an' send it,
            As soon 's he smells 't,
Baith their disease and what will mend it,
            At once he tells 't.

XX

"And then a' doctor's saws and whittles
Of a' dimensions, shapes, an' mettles,
A' kinds o' boxes, mugs, and bottles,
            He 's sure to hae:
Their Latin names as fast he rattles
            As A B C.

XXI

"Calces o' fossils, earth, and trees;
True *sal-marinum* o' the seas;
The *farina* of beans an' pease,
            He has 't in plenty;
Aqua-fontis, what you please,
            He can content ye.

XXII

"Forbye some new, uncommon weapons,
Urinus spiritus of capons;
Or mite-horn shavings, filings, scrapings
            Distill'd *per se;*
Sal-alkali o' midge-tail-clippings,
            And monie mae."

XXIII

"Waes me for Johnie Ged's Hole now,"
Quoth I, "if that thae news be true!
His braw calf-ward whare gowans grew
            Sae white and bonie,
Nae doubt they 'll rive it wi' the plew:
            They 'll ruin Johnie!"

XXIV

The creature grain'd an eldritch laugh,
And says: "Ye nedna yoke the pleugh,
Kirkyards will soon be till'd eneugh,
          Tak ye nae fear:
They 'll a' be trench'd wi monie a sheugh
          In twa-three year.

XXV

"Whare I kill'd ane, a fair strae death
By loss o' blood or want o' breath,
This night I 'm free to tak my aith,
          That Hornbrook's skill
Has clad a score i' their last claith
          By drap an' pill.

XXVI

"An honest wabster to his trade,
Whase wife's twa nieves were scarce weel-bred,
Gat tippence-worth to mend her head,
          When it was sair;
The wife slade cannie to her bed,
          But ne'er spak mair.

XXVII

"A countra laird had taen the batts,
Or some curmurring in his guts,
His only son for Hornbook sets,
          An' pays him well:
The lad, for twa guid gimmer-pets,
          Was laird himsel.

XXVIII

"A bonie lass—ye kend her name—
Some ill-brewn drink had hov'd her wame;
She trusts hersel, to hide the shame,
                    In Hornbook's care;
Horn sent her aff to her lang hame
                    To hide it there.

XXIX

"That's just a swatch o' Hornbook's way;
Thus goes he on from day to day,
Thus does he poison, kill, an' slay,
                    An's weel paid for't;
Yet stops me o' my lawfu' prey
                    Wi' his damn'd dirt:

XXX

"But, hark! I'll tell you of a plot,
Tho' dinna ye be speakin o't:
I'll nail the self-conceited sot,
                    As dead's a herrin;
Niest time we meet, I'll wad a groat,
                    He gets his fairin!"

XXXI

But just as he began to tell,
The auld kirk-hammer strak the bell
Some wee short hour ayont the twal,
                    Which raised us baith:
I took the way that pleas'd mysel,
                    And sae did Death.

The Ordination

For sense, they little owe to frugal Heav'n:
To please the mob they hide the little giv'n.

I

Kilmarnock wabsters, fidge an' claw,
    An' pour your creeshie nations;
An' ye wha leather rax an' draw,
    Of a' denominations;
Swith! to the Laigh Kirk, ane an' a',
    An' there tak up your stations;
Then aff to Begbie's in a raw,
    An' pour divine libations
                    For joy this day.

II

Curst Common-sense, that imp o' hell,
    Cam in wi' *Maggie Lauder:*
But Oliphant aft made her yell,
    An' Russell sair misca'd her:
This day Mackinlay taks the flail,
    An' he's the boy will blaud her!
He'll clap a shangan on her tail,
    An' set the bairns to daud her
                    Wi' dirt this day.

III

Mak haste an' turn King David owre,
    An' lilt wi' holy clangor;
O' double verse come gie us four,
    An' skirl up the *Bangor:*
This day the Kirk kicks up a stoure:
    Nae mair the knaves shall wrang her,

For Heresy is in her pow'r,
   And gloriously she 'll whang her
                Wi' pith this day.

IV

Come, let a proper text be read,
   An' touch it aff wi' vigour,
How graceless Ham leugh at his dad,
   Which made Canaan a nigger;
Or Phineas drove the murdering blade
   Wi' whore-abhorring rigour;
Or Zipporah, the scauldin jad,
   Was like a bluidy tiger
                I' th' inn that day.

V

There, try his mettle on the Creed,
   And bind him down wi' caution,—
That stipend is a carnal weed
   He taks but for the fashion—
And gie him o'er the flock to feed,
   And punish each transgression;
Especial, rams that cross the breed,
   Gie them sufficient threshin:
                Spare them nae day.

VI

Now auld Kilmarnock, cock thy tail,
   An' toss thy horns fu' canty;
Nae mair thou 'lt rowte out-owre the dale,
   Because thy pasture 's scanty;
For lapfu's large o' gospel kail
   Shall fill thy crib in plenty,

An' runts o' grace, the pick an' wale,
  No gien by way o' dainty,
              But ilka day.

VII

Nae mair by Babel's streams we'll weep
  To think upon our Zion;
And hing our fiddles up to sleep,
  Like baby-clouts a-dryin.
Come, screw the pegs wi' tunefu' cheep,
  And o'er the thairms be tryin;
O, rare! to see our elbucks wheep,
  And a' like lamb-tails flyin
              Fu' fast this day!

VIII

Lang, Patronage, wi' rod o' airn,
  Has shor'd the Kirk's undoin;
As lately Fenwick, sair forfairn,
  Has proven to its ruin:
Our patron, honest man! Glencairn,
  He saw mischief was brewin;
An' like a godly, elect bairn,
  He's waled us out a true ane,
              And sound this day.

IX

Now, Robertson, harangue nae mair,
  But steek your gab for ever;
Or try the wicked town of Ayr,
  For there they'll think you clever;
Or, nae reflection on your lear,
  Ye may commence a shaver;

Or to the Netherton repair,
    An' turn a carpet-weaver
                    Aff-hand this day.

X

Mu'trie and you were just a match,
    We never had sic twa drones:
Auld Hornie did the Laigh Kirk watch,
    Just like a winkin baudrons,
And ay he catch'd the tither wretch,
    To fry them in his caudrons;
But now his Honor maun detach,
    Wi' a' his brimstone squadrons,
                    Fast, fast this day.

XI

See, see auld Orthodoxy's faes
    She's swingein thro' the city!
Hark, how the nine-tailed cat she plays!
    I vow it's unco pretty;
There, Learning, with his Greekish face,
    Grunts out some Latin ditty;
And Common-Sense is gaun, she says,
    To mak to Jamie Beattie
                    Her plaint this day.

XII

But there's Morality himsel,
    Embracing all opinions;
Hear, how he gies the tither yell
    Between his twa companions!
See, how she peels the skin an' fell,
    As ane were peelin onions!

Now there, they 're packèd aff to hell,
    An' banish'd our dominions,
                    Henceforth this day.

XIII

O happy day! rejoice, rejoice!
    Come bouse about the porter!
Morality's demure decoys
    Shall here nae mair find quarter:
Mackinlay, Russell, are the boys
    That Heresy can torture;
They 'll gie her on a rape a hoyse,
    And cowe her measure shorter
                    By th' head some day.

XIV

Come, bring the tither mutchkin in,
    And here 's—for a conclusion—
To ev'ry New Light mother's son,
    From this time forth, confusion!
If mair they deave us wi' their din
    Or patronage intrusion,
We 'll light a spunk, and ev'ry skin
    We 'll run them aff in fusion,
                    Like oil some day.

Address to a Haggis

I

Fair fa' your honest, sonsie face,
Great chieftain o' the puddin-race!

Aboon them a' ye tak your place,
                    Painch, tripe, or thairm:
Weel are ye wordy of a grace
                    As lang's my arm.

II

The groaning trencher there ye fill,
Your hurdies like a distant hill,
Your pin wad help to mend a mill
                    In time o' need,
While thro' your pores the dews distil
                    Like amber bead.

III

His knife see rustic Labour dight,
An' cut ye up wi' ready slight,
Trenching your gushing entrails bright,
                    Like onie ditch;
And then, O what a glorious sight,
                    Warm-reekin, rich!

IV

Then, horn for horn, they stretch an' strive:
Deil tak the hindmost, on they drive,
Till a' their weel-swall'd kytes belyve
                    Are bent like drums;
Then auld Guidman, maist like to rive,
                    "Bethankit!" hums.

V

Is there that owre his French *ragout,*
Or *olio* that wad staw a sow,
Or *fricassee* wad mak her spew
                    Wi' perfect sconner,

Looks down wi' sneering, scornfu' view
           On sic a dinner?

VI

Poor devil! see him owre his trash,
As feckless as a wither'd rash,
His spindle shank a guid whip–lash,
           His nieve a nit;
Thro' bluidy flood or field to dash,
           O how unfit!

VII

But mark the Rustic, haggis-fed,
The trembling earth resounds his tread,
Clap in his walie nieve a blade,
           He 'll make it whissle;
An' legs, an' arms, an' heads will sned
           Like taps o' thrissle.

VIII

Ye Pow'rs, wha mak mankind your care,
And dish them out their bill o' fare,
Auld Scotland wants nae skinking ware,
           That jaups in luggies;
But, if ye wish her gratefu' prayer,
           Gie her a Haggis!

FROM THE EDINBURGH EDITION, 1793

Tam o' Shanter

A Tale

Of Brownyis and of Bogillis full is this Buke.
—GAWIN DOUGLAS

When chapman billies leave the street,
And drouthy neebors neebors meet;
As market-days are wearing late,
An' folk begin to tak the gate;
While we sit bousing at the nappy,
An' getting fou and unco happy,
We think na on the lang Scots miles,
The mosses, waters, slaps, and styles,
That lie between us and our hame,
Whare sits our sulky, sullen dame,
Gathering her brows like gathering storm,
Nursing her wrath to keep it warm.

This truth fand honest Tam o' Shanter,
As he frae Ayr ae night did canter:
(Auld Ayr, wham ne'er a town surpasses,
For honest men and bonie lasses).

O Tam, had'st thou but been sae wise,
As taen thy ain wife Kate's advice!
She tauld thee weel thou was a skellum,
A blethering, blustering, drunken blellum;

That frae November till October,
Ae market-day thou was nae sober;
That ilka melder wi' the miller,
Thou sat as lang as thou had siller;
That ev'ry naig was ca'd a shoe on,
The smith and thee gat roaring fou on;
That at the Lord's house, even on Sunday,
Thou drank wi' Kirkton Jean till Monday.
She prophesied, that, late or soon,
Thou would be found deep drown'd in Doon,
Or catch'd wi' warlocks in the mirk
By Alloway's auld, haunted kirk.

Ah! gentle dames, it gars me greet,
To think how monie counsels sweet,
How monie lengthen'd, sage advices
The husband frae the wife despises!

But to our tale: Ae market-night,
Tam had got planted unco right,
Fast by an ingle, bleezing finely,
Wi' reaming swats, that drank divinely;
And at his elbow, Souter Johnie,
His ancient, trusty, drouthy cronie:
Tam lo'ed him like a very brither;
They had been fou for weeks thegither.
The night drave on wi' sangs and clatter;
And ay the ale was growing better:
The landlady and Tam grew gracious
Wi' secret favours, sweet and precious:
The Souter tauld his queerest stories;
The landlord's laugh was ready chorus:
The storm without might rair and rustle,
Tam did na mind the storm a whistle.

Care, mad to see a man sae happy,
E'en drown'd himsel amang the nappy.
As bees flee hame wi' lades o' treasure,
The minutes wing'd their way wi' pleasure:
Kings may be blest but Tam was glorious,
O'er a' the ills o' life victorious!

But pleasures are like poppies spread:
You seize the flow'r, its bloom is shed;
Or like the snow falls in the river,
A moment white—then melts for ever;
Or like the borealis race,
That flit ere you can point their place;
Or like the rainbow's lovely form
Evanishing amid the storm.
Nae man can tether time or tide;
The hour approaches Tam maun ride:
That hour, o' night's black arch the keystane,
That dreary hour Tam mounts his beast in;
And sic a night he taks the road in,
As ne'er poor sinner was abroad in.

The wind blew as 't wad blawn its last;
The rattling showers rose on the blast;
The speedy gleams the darkness swallow'd;
Loud, deep, and lang the thunder bellow'd:
That night, a child might understand,
The Deil had business on his hand.

Weel mounted on his gray mare Meg,
A better never lifted leg,
Tam skelpit on thro' dub and mire,
Despising wind, and rain, and fire;
Whiles holding fast his guid blue bonnet,

Whiles crooning o'er some auld Scots sonnet,
Whiles glow'ring round wi' prudent cares,
Lest bogles catch him unawares:
Kirk-Alloway was drawing nigh,
Whare ghaists and houlets nightly cry.

By this time he was cross the ford,
Whare in the snaw the chapman smoor'd;
And past the birks and meikle stane,
Whare drunken Charlie brak 's neck-bane;
And thro' the whins, and by the cairn,
Whare hunters fand the murder'd bairn;
And near the thorn, aboon the well,
Whare Mungo's mither hang'd hersel.
Before him Doon pours all his floods;
The doubling storm roars thro' the woods;
The lightnings flash from pole to pole;
Near and more near the thunders roll:
When, glimmering thro' the groaning trees,
Kirk-Alloway seem'd in a bleeze,
Thro' ilka bore the beams were glancing,
And loud resounded mirth and dancing.

Inspiring bold John Barleycorn,
What dangers thou canst make us scorn!
Wi' tippenny, we fear nae evil;
Wi' usquabae, we'll face the Devil!
The swats sae ream'd in Tammie's noddle,
Fair play, he car'd na deils a boddle.
But Maggie stood, right sair astonish'd,
Till, by the heel and hand admonish'd,
She ventur'd forward on the light;
And, vow! Tam saw an unco sight!

Warlocks and witches in a dance:
Nae cotillion, brent new frae France,
But hornpipes, jigs, strathspeys, and reels,
Put life and mettle in their heels.
A winnock-bunker in the east,
There sat Auld Nick, in shape o' beast;
A tousie tyke, black, grim, and large,
To gie them music was his charge:
He screw'd the pipes and gart them skirl,
Till roof and rafters a' did dirl.
Coffins stood round, like open presses,
That shaw'd the dead in their last dresses;
And, by some devilish cantraip sleight,
Each in its cauld hand held a light:
By which heroic Tam was able
To note upon the haly table,
A murderer's banes, in gibbet-airns;
Twa span-lang, wee, unchristen'd bairns;
A thief new-cutted frae a rape—
Wi' his last gasp his gab did gape;
Five tomahawks wi' bluid red-rusted;
Five scymitars wi' murder crusted;
A garter which a babe had strangled;
A knife a father's throat had mangled—
Whom his ain son o' life bereft—
The grey-hairs yet stack to the heft;
Wi' mair of horrible and awefu',
Which even to name wad be unlawfu'.

As Tammie glowr'd, amaz'd, and curious,
The mirth and fun grew fast and furious;
The piper loud and louder blew,
The dancers quick and quicker flew,
They reel'd, they set, they cross'd, they cleekit,

Till ilka carlin swat and reekit,
And coost her duddies to the wark,
And linket at it in her sark!

Now Tam, O Tam! had thae been queans,
A' plump and strapping in their teens!
Their sarks, instead o' creeshie flannen,
Been snaw-white seventeen hunder linen!—
Thir breeks o' mine, my only pair,
That ance were plush, o' guid blue hair,
I wad hae gi'en them off my hurdies
For ae blink o' the bonie burdies!

But wither'd beldams, auld and droll,
Rigwoodie hags wad spean a foal,
Louping and flinging on a crummock,
I wonder did na turn thy stomach!

But Tam kend what was what fu' brawlie:
There was ae winsome wench and wawlie,
That night enlisted in the core,
Lang after kend on Carrick shore
(For monie a beast to dead she shot,
An' perish'd monie a bonie boat,
And shook baith meikle corn and bear,
And kept the country-side in fear).
Her cutty sark, o' Paisley harn,
That while a lassie she had worn,
In longitude tho' sorely scanty,
It was her best, and she was vauntie. . . .
Ah! little kend thy reverend grannie,
That sark she coft for her wee Nannie,
Wi' twa pund Scots ('t was a' her riches),
Wad ever grac'd a dance of witches!

But here my Muse her wing maun cour,
Sic flights are far beyond her power:
To sing how Nannie lap and flang
(A souple jad she was and strang),
And how Tam stood like ane bewitch'd,
And thought his very een enrich'd;
Even Satan glowr'd, and fidg'd fu' fain,
And hotch'd and blew wi' might and main;
Till first ae caper, syne anither,
Tam tint his reason a' thegither,
And roars out: "Weel done, Cutty-sark!"
And in an instant all was dark;
And scarcely had he Maggie rallied,
When out the hellish legion sallied.

As bees bizz out wi' angry fyke,
When plundering herds assail their byke;
As open pussie's mortal foes,
When, pop! she starts before their nose;
As eager runs the market-crowd,
When "Catch the thief!" resounds aloud:
So Maggie runs, the witches follow,
Wi' monie an eldritch skriech and hollo.

Ah, Tam! ah, Tam! thou 'll get thy fairin!
In hell they 'll roast thee like a herrin!
In vain thy Kate awaits thy comin!
Kate soon will be a woefu' woman!
Now, do thy speedy utmost, Meg,
And win the key-stane of the brig;
There, at them thou thy tail may toss,
A running stream they dare na cross!
But ere the key-stane she could make,
The fient a tail she had to shake;

For Nannie, far before the rest,
Hard upon noble Maggie prest,
And flew at Tam wi' furious ettle;
But little wist she Maggie's mettle!
Ae spring brought off her master hale,
But left behind her ain grey tail:
The carlin claught her by the rump,
And left poor Maggie scarce a stump.

Now, wha this tale o' truth shall read,
Ilk man, and mother's son, take heed:
Whene'er to drink you are inclin'd,
Or cutty sarks run in your mind,
Think! ye may buy the joys o'er dear:
Remember Tam o' Shanter's mare.

POSTHUMOUS PIECES

The Jolly Beggars

A Cantata

RECITATIVO

I

When lyart leaves bestrow the yird,
Or, wavering like the bauckie-bird,
  Bedim cauld Boreas' blast;
When hailstanes drive wi' bitter skyte,
And infant frosts begin to bite,
  In hoary cranreuch drest;

Ae night at e'en a merry core
    O' randie, gangrel bodies
In Poosie-Nansie's held the splore,
    To drink their orra duddies:
        Wi' quaffing and laughing
            They ranted an' they sang,
        Wi' jumping an' thumping
            The vera girdle rang.

II

First, niest the fire, in auld red rags
Ane sat, weel brac'd wi' mealy bags
    And knapsack a' in order;
His doxy lay within his arm;
Wi' usquebae an' blankets warm,
    She blinket on her sodger.
An' ay he gies the tozie drab
    The tither skelpin kiss,
While she held up her greedy gab
    Just like an aumous dish:
        Ilk smack still did crack still
            Like onie cadger's whup;
        Then, swaggering an' staggering,
            He roar'd this ditty up:—

AIR

TUNE: *"Soldier's Joy"*

I

I am a son of Mars, who have been in many wars,
    And show my cuts and scars wherever I come:

This here was for a wench, and that other in a trench
    When welcoming the French at the sound of the drum.
                          Lal de daudle, etc.

II

My prenticeship I past, where my leader breath'd his last,
    When the bloody die was cast on the heights of Abram;
And I servèd out my trade when the gallant game was play'd,
    And the Moro low was laid at the sound of the drum.

III

I lastly was with Curtis among the floating batt'ries,
    And there I left for witness an arm and a limb;
Yet let my country need me, with Eliott to head me
    I'd clatter on my stumps at the sound of the drum.

IV

And now, tho' I must beg with a wooden arm and leg
    And many a tatter'd rag hanging over my bum,
I'm as happy with my wallet, my bottle, and my callet
    As when I us'd in scarlet to follow a drum.

V

What tho' with hoary locks I must stand the winter shocks,
    Beneath the woods and rocks oftentimes for a home?
When the tother bag I sell, and the tother bottle tell,
    I could meet a troop of Hell at the sound of a drum.
                          Lal de daudle, etc.

He ended; and the kebars sheuk
   Aboon the chorus roar;
While frighted rattons backward leuk,
   An' seek the benmost bore:
A fairy fiddler frae the neuk,
   He skirl'd out *Encore!*
But up arose the martial chuck,
   An' laid the loud uproar:—

AIR

TUNE: *"Sodger Laddie"*

I

I once was a maid, tho' I cannot tell when,
And still my delight is in proper young men.
Some one of a troop of dragoons was my daddie:
No wonder I'm fond of a sodger laddie!
                Sing, lal de dal, etc.

II

The first of my loves was a swaggering blade:
To rattle the thundering drum was his trade;
His leg was so tight, and his cheek was so ruddy,
Transported I was with my sodger laddie.

III

But the godly old chaplain left him in the lurch;
The sword I forsook for the sake of the church;
He riskèd the soul, and I ventur'd the body:
'T was then I prov'd false to my sodger laddie.

IV

Full soon I grew sick of my sanctified sot;
The regiment at large for a husband I got;
From the gilded spontoon to the fife I was ready:
I askèd no more but a sodger laddie.

V

But the Peace it reduc'd me to beg in despair,
Till I met my old boy in a Cunningham Fair;
His rags regimental they flutter'd so gaudy:
My heart it rejoic'd at a sodger laddie.

VI

And now I have liv'd—I know not how long!
But still I can join in a cup and a song;
And whilst with both hands I can hold the glass steady,
Here's to thee, my hero, my sodger laddie!
      Sing, lal de dal, etc.

RECITATIVO

Poor Merry-Andrew in the neuk
    Sat guzzling wi' a tinkler-hizzie;
They mind 't na wha the chorus teuk,
    Between themselves they were sae busy.
    At length, wi' drink an' courting dizzy,
He stoiter'd up an' made a face;
    Then turn'd an' laid a smack on Grizzie,
Syne tun'd his pipes wi' grave grimace:—

I

Sir Wisdom's a fool when he's fou;
    Sir Knave is a fool in a session:
He's there but a prentice I trow,
    But I am a fool by profession.

II

My grannie she bought me a beuk,
    An' I held awa to the school:
I fear I my talent misteuk,
    But what will ye hae of a fool?

III

For drink I wad venture my neck;
    A hizzie's the half of my craft:
But what could ye other expect
    Of ane that's avowedly daft?

IV

I ance was tyed up like a stirk
    For civilly swearing and quaffing;
I ance was abus'd i' the kirk
    For towsing a lass i' my daffin.

V

Poor Andrew that tumbles for sport
    Let naebody name wi' a jeer:
There's even, I'm tauld, i' the Court
    A tumbler ca'd the Premier.

VI

Observ'd ye yon reverend lad
  Mak faces to tickle the mob?
He rails at our mountebank squad—
  It's rivalship just i' the job!

VII

And now my conclusion I'll tell,
  For faith! I'm confoundedly dry:
The chiel that's a fool for himsel,
  Guid Lord! he's far dafter than I.

RECITATIVO

Then niest outspak a raucle carlin,
Wha kent fu' weel to cleek the sterlin,
For monie a pursie she had hookèd,
An' had in monie a well been doukèd.
Her love had been a Highland laddie,
But weary fa' the waefu' woodie!
Wi' sighs an' sobs she thus began
To wail her braw John Highlandman:—

AIR

TUNE: *"O an' Ye Were Dead, Guidman"*

I

A Highland lad my love was born,
The Lalland laws he held in scorn,
But he still was faithfu' to his clan,
My gallant, braw John Highlandman.

Sing hey my braw John Highlandman!
Sing ho my braw John Highlandman!
There's not a lad in a' the lan'
Was match for my John Highlandman!

II

With his philibeg, an' tartan plaid,
An' guid claymore down by his side,
The ladies' hearts he did trepan,
My gallant, braw John Highlandman.

III

We rangèd a' from Tweed to Spey,
An' liv'd like lords an' ladies gay,
For a Lalland face he fearèd none,
My gallant, braw John Highlandman.

IV

They banish'd him beyond the sea,
But ere the bud was on the tree,
Adown my cheeks the pearls ran,
Embracing my John Highlandman.

V

But, Och! they catch'd him at the last,
And bound him in a dungeon fast.
My curse upon them every one—
They 've hang'd my braw John Highland man!

VI

And now a widow I must mourn
The pleasures that will ne'er return;

No comfort but a hearty can
When I think on John Highlandman.

CHORUS

Sing hey my braw John Highlandman!
Sing ho my braw John Highlandman!
There's not a lad in a' the lan'
Was match for my John Highlandman!

RECITATIVO

I

A pigmy scraper on a fiddle,
Wha us'd to trystes an' fairs to driddle,
Her strappin limb an' gawsie middle
         (He reach'd nae higher)
Had hol'd his heartie like a riddle,
         An' blawn 't on fire.

II

Wi' hand on hainch and upward e'e,
He croon'd his gamut, one, two, three,
Then in an *arioso* key
         The wee Apollo
Set off wi' *allegretto* glee
         His *giga* solo:—

TUNE: *"Whistle Owre the Lave O 't"*

I

Let me ryke up to dight that tear;
An' go wi' me an' be my dear,
An' then your every care an' fear
   May whistle owre the lave o 't.

CHORUS

I am a fiddler to my trade,
An' a' the tunes that e'er I play'd,
The sweetest still to wife or maid
   Was *Whistle Owre the Lave O 't.*

II

At kirns an' weddins we 'se be there,
An' O, sae nicely 's we will fare!
We 'll bowse about till Daddie Care
   Sing *Whistle Owre the Lave O 't.*

III

Sae merrily the banes we 'll pyke,
An' sun oursels about the dyke;
An' at our leisure, when ye like,
   We 'll—whistle owre the lave o 't!

IV

But bless me wi' your heav'n o' charms,
An' while I kittle hair on thairms,

Hunger, cauld, an' a' sic harms
   May whistle owre the lave o 't.

CHORUS

I am a fiddler to my trade,
An' a' the tunes that e'er I play'd,
The sweetest still to wife or maid
   Was *Whistle Owre the Lave O 't.*

RECITATIVO

I

Her charms had struck a sturdy caird
   As weel as poor gut-scraper;
He taks the fiddler by the beard,
   An' draws a roosty rapier;
He swoor by a' was swearing worth
   To speet him like a pliver,
Unless he would from that time forth
   Relinquish her for ever.

II

Wi' ghastly e'e poor Tweedle-Dee
   Upon his hunkers bended,
An' pray'd for grace wi' ruefu' face,
   An' sae the quarrel ended.
But tho' his little heart did grieve
   When round the tinkler prest her,
He feign'd to snirtle in his sleeve
   When thus the caird address'd her:—

TUNE: *"Clout the Cauldron"*

I

My bonie lass, I work in brass,
  A tinkler is my station;
I've travell'd round all Christian ground
  In this my occupation;
I've taen the gold, an' been enrolled
  In many a noble squadron;
But vain they search'd when off I march'd
  To go an' clout the cauldron.

II

Despise that shrimp, that wither'd imp,
  With a' his noise an' cap'rin,
An' take a share wi' those that bear
  The budget and the apron!
And by that stowp, my faith an' houpe!
  And by that dear Kilbaigie!
If e'er ye want, or meet wi' scant,
  May I ne'er weet my craigie!

RECITATIVO

I

The caird prevail'd: th' unblushing fair
  In his embraces sunk,
Partly wi' love o'ercome sae sair,
  An' partly she was drunk.
Sir Violino, with an air
  That show'd a man o' spunk,

Wish'd unison between the pair,
   An' made the bottle clunk
               To their health that night.

II

But hurchin Cupid shot a shaft,
   That play'd a dame a shavie:
The fiddler rak'd her fore and aft
   Behint the chicken cavie;
Her lord, a wight of Homer's craft,
   Tho' limpin' wi' the spavie,
He hirpl'd up, an' lap like daft,
   An' shor'd them "Dainty Davie"
               O' boot that night.

III

He was a care-defying blade
   As ever Bacchus listed!
Tho' Fortune sair upon him laid,
   His heart, she ever miss'd it.
He had no wish but—to be glad,
   Nor want but—when he thristed,
He hated nought but—to be sad;
   An' thus the Muse suggested
               His sang that night.

AIR

TUNE: *"For a' That, an' a' That"*

I

I am a Bard, of no regard
   Wi' gentle folks an' a' that,

But Homer-like the glowrin byke,
   Frae town to town I draw that.

For a' that, an' a' that,
   An' twice as muckle 's a' that,
I 've lost but ane, I 've twa behin',
   I 've wife eneugh for a' that.

II

I never drank the Muses' stank,
   Castalia's burn, an' a' that;
But there it streams, an' richly reams—
   My Helicon I ca' that.

III

Great love I bear to a' the fair,
   Their humble slave an' a' that;
But lordly will, I hold it still
   A mortal sin to thraw that.

IV

In raptures sweet this hour we meet
   Wi' mutual love an' a' that;
But for how lang the flie may stang,
   Let inclination law that!

V

Their tricks an' craft hae put me daft,
   They 've taen me in, an' a' that;
But clear your decks, an' here 's the Sex!
   I like the jads for a' that.

78 | THE ESSENTIAL BURNS

For a' that, an' a that,
　　An' twice as muckle 's a' that,
My dearest bluid, to do them guid,
　　They 're welcome till 't for a' that!

RECITATIVO

So sung the Bard, and Nansie's wa's
Shook with a thunder of applause,
　　Re-echo'd from each mouth!
They toom'd their pocks, they pawn'd their duds,
They scarcely left to coor their fuds,
　　To quench their lowin drouth.
Then owre again the jovial thrang
　　The Poet did request
To lowse his pack, an' wale a sang,
　　A ballad o' the best:
　　　　He rising, rejoicing
　　　　　Between his twa Deborahs,
　　　　Looks round him, an' found them
　　　　　Impatient for the chorus:—

AIR

TUNE: *"Jolly Mortals, Fill Your Glasses"*

I

See the smoking bowl before us!
　Mark our jovial, ragged ring!

Round and round take up the chorus,
  And in raptures let us sing:

CHORUS

A fig for those by law protected!
  Liberty's a glorious feast,
Courts for cowards were erected,
  Churches built to please the priest!

II

What is title, what is treasure,
  What is reputation's care?
If we lead a life of pleasure,
  'T is no matter how or where!

III

With the ready trick and fable
  Round we wander all the day;
And at night in barn or stable
  Hug our doxies on the hay.

IV

Does the train-attended carriage
  Thro' the country lighter rove?
Does the sober bed of marriage
  Witness brighter scenes of love?

V

Life is all a variorum,
  We regard not how it goes;
Let them prate about decorum,
  Who have character to lose.

Here's to budgets, bags, and wallets!
　Here's to all the wandering train!
Here's our ragged brats and callets!
　One and all, cry out, Amen!

CHORUS

A fig for those by law protected!
　Liberty's a glorious feast,
Courts for cowards were erected,
　Churches built to please the priest!

Holy Willie's Prayer

And send the godly in a pet to pray.
—POPE

I

O Thou that in the Heavens does dwell,
Wha, as it pleases best Thysel,
Sends ane to Heaven an' ten to Hell
　　　　A' for Thy glory,
And no for onie guid or ill
　　　　They've done before Thee!

II

I bless and praise Thy matchless might,
When thousands Thou hast left in night,
That I am here before Thy sight,
　　　　For gifts an' grace

A burning and a shining light
                    To a' this place.

III

What was I, or my generation,
That I should get sic exaltation?
I, wha deserv'd most just damnation
                    For broken laws
Sax thousand years ere my creation,
                    Thro' Adam's cause!

IV

When from my mither's womb I fell,
Thou might hae plung'd me deep in hell
To gnash my gooms, and weep, and wail
                    In burning lakes,
Whare damnèd devils roar and yell,
                    Chain'd to their stakes.

V

Yet I am here, a chosen sample,
To show Thy grace is great and ample:
I'm here a pillar o' Thy temple,
                    Strong as a rock,
A guide, a buckler, and example
                    To a' Thy flock!

VI

But yet, O Lord! confess I must:
At times I'm fash'd wi' fleshly lust;
An' sometimes, too, in warldly trust,
                    Vile self gets in;
But Thou remembers we are dust,
                    Defiled wi' sin.

VII

O Lord! yestreen, Thou kens, wi' Meg—
Thy pardon I sincerely beg—
O, may 't ne'er be a living plague
        To my dishonour!
An' I 'll ne'er lift a lawless leg
        Again upon her.

VIII

Besides, I farther maun avow—
Wi' Leezie's lass, three times, I trow—
But, Lord, that Friday I was fou,
        When I cam near her,
Or else, Thou kens, Thy servant true
        Wad never steer her.

IX

Maybe Thou lets this fleshly thorn
Buffet Thy servant e'en and morn,
Lest he owre proud and high should turn
        That he's sae gifted:
If sae, Thy han' maun e'en be borne
        Until Thou lift it.

X

Lord, bless Thy chosen in this place,
For here Thou has a chosen race!
But God confound their stubborn face
        An' blast their name,
Wha bring Thy elders to disgrace
        An' open shame!

XI

Lord, mind Gau'n Hamilton's deserts:
He drinks, an' swears, an' plays at cartes,
Yet has sae monie takin arts
          Wi' great and sma',
Frae God's ain Priest the people's hearts
            He steals awa.

XII

And when we chasten'd him therefore,
Thou kens how he bred sic a splore,
And set the warld in a roar
          O' laughin at us:
Curse Thou his basket and his store,
            Kail an' potatoes!

XIII

Lord, hear my earnest cry and pray'r
Against that Presbyt'ry of Ayr!
Thy strong right hand, Lord, mak it bare
          Upo' their heads!
Lord, visit them, an' dinna spare,
            For their misdeeds!

XIV

O Lord, my God! that glib-tongu'd Aiken,
My vera heart and flesh are quakin
To think how we stood sweatin, shakin,
          An' pish'd wi' dread,
While he, wi' hingin lip an' snakin,
            Held up his head.

XV

Lord, in Thy day o' vengeance try him!
Lord, visit him wha did employ him!
And pass not in Thy mercy by them,
                    Nor hear their pray'r,
But for Thy people's sake destroy them,
                    An' dinna spare!

XVI

But, Lord, remember me and mine
Wi' mercies temporal and divine,
That I for grace an' gear may shine
                    Excell'd by nane;
And a' the glory shall be Thine—
                    Amen, Amen!

A Poet's Welcome
to His Love-Begotten Daughter

THE FIRST INSTANCE
THAT ENTITLED HIM TO THE VENERABLE
APPELLATION OF FATHER

I

Thou 's welcome, wean! Mishanter fa' me,
If thoughts o' thee or yet thy mammie
Shall ever daunton me or awe me,
                    My sweet, wee lady,
Or if I blush when thou shalt ca' me
                    Tyta or daddie!

II

What tho' they ca' me fornicator,
An' tease my name in kintra clatter?
The mair they talk, I'm kend the better;
        E'en let them clash!
An auld wife's tongue's a feckless matter
        To gie ane fash.

III

Welcome, my bonie, sweet, wee dochter!
Tho' ye come here a wee unsought for,
And tho' your comin I hae fought for
        Baith kirk and queir;
Yet, by my faith, ye're no unwrought for—
        That I shall swear!

IV

Sweet fruit o' monie a merry dint,
My funny toil is no a' tint:
Tho' thou cam to the warl' asklent,
        Which fools may scoff at,
In my last plack thy part's be in't
        The better half o't.

V

Tho' I should be the waur bestead,
Thou's be as braw and bienly clad,
And thy young years as nicely bred
        Wi' education,
As onie brat o' wedlock's bed
        In a' thy station.

VI

Wee image o' my bonie Betty,
As fatherly I kiss and daut thee,
As dear and near my heart I set thee,
                      Wi' as guid will,
As a' the priests had seen me get thee
                      That's out o' Hell.

VII

Gude grant that thou may ay inherit
Thy mither's looks an' gracefu' merit,
An' thy poor, worthless daddie's spirit
                      Without his failins!
'T will please me mair to see thee heir it
                      Than stocket mailins.

VIII

And if thou be what I wad hae thee,
An' tak the counsel I shall gie thee,
I'll never rue my trouble wi' thee—
                      The cost nor shame o 't—
But be a loving father to thee,
                      And brag the name o 't.

On Captain Grose

WRITTEN ON AN ENVELOPE ENCLOSING
A LETTER TO HIM

I

Ken ye ought o' Captain Grose?
                Igo and ago

If he 's among his friends or foes?
>*Iram, coram, dago*

II

Is he south, or is he north?
>*Igo and ago*
Or drownèd in the River Forth?
>*Iram, coram, dago*

III

Is he slain by Hielan' bodies?
>*Igo and ago*
And eaten like a wether haggis?
>*Iram, coram, dago*

IV

Is he to Abra'm's bosom gane?
>*Igo and ago*
Or haudin Sarah by the wame?
>*Iram, coram, dago*

V

Where'er he be, the Lord be near him!
>*Igo and ago*
As for the Deil, he daur na steer him.
>*Iram, coram, dago*

VI

But please transmit th' enclosèd letter
>*Igo and ago*
Which will oblige your humble debtor
>*Iram, coram, dago*

So may ye hae auld stanes in store,
   Igo and ago
The very stanes that Adam bore!
   Iram, coram, dago

VIII

So may ye get in glad possession,
   Igo and ago
The coins o' Satan's coronation!
   Iram, coram, dago

The Trogger

TUNE: *"Buy Broom Besoms"*

CHORUS

Buy braw troggin
 Frae the banks o' Dee!
Wha wants troggin
 Let him come to me!

I

Wha will buy my troggin,
 Fine election ware,
Broken trade o' Broughton,
 A' in high repair?

II

There 's a noble Earl's
 Fame and high renown,

For an auld sang—it 's thought
   The guids were stown.

III
Here 's the worth o' Broughton
   In a needle's e'e.
Here 's a reputation
   Tint by Balmaghie.

IV
Here 's its stuff and lining,
   Cardoness's head—
Fine for a soger,
   A' the wale o' lead.

V
Here 's a little wadset—
   Buittle's scrap o' truth,
Pawn'd in a gin-shop,
   Quenching holy drouth.

VI
Here 's an honest conscience
   Might a prince adorn,
Frae the downs o' Tinwald—
   So was never worn!

VII
Here 's armorial bearings
   Frae the manse o' Urr:
The crest, a sour crab-apple
   Rotten at the core.

VIII

Here is Satan's picture,
  Like a bizzard gled
Pouncing poor Redcastle,
  Sprawlin like a taed.

IX

Here's the font where Douglas
  Stane and mortar names,
Lately used at Caily
  Christening Murray's crimes.

X

Here's the worth and wisdom
  Collieston can boast:
By a thievish midge
  They had been nearly lost.

XI

Here is Murray's fragments
  O' the Ten Commands,
Gifted by Black Jock
  To get them aff his hands.

XII

Saw ye e'er sic troggin?—
  If to buy ye're slack,
Hornie's turnin chapman:
  He'll buy a' the pack!

Buy braw troggin
   Frae the banks o' Dee
Wha wants troggin
   Let him come to me!

At Carron Ironworks

WRITTEN ON THE WINDOW OF THE INN AT CARRON

We cam na here to view your warks
   In hopes to be mair wise,
But only, lest we gang to Hell,
   It may be nae surprise.

But when we tirl'd at your door
   Your porter dought na bear us:
Saw may, should we to Hell's yetts come,
   Your billie Satan sair us.

FROM JOHNSON'S *MUSICAL MUSEUM*

O, Whistle an' I'll Come to Ye, My Lad

CHORUS

O, whistle an' I'll come to ye, my lad!
O, whistle an' I'll come to ye, my lad!
Tho' father an' mother an' a' should gae mad,
O, whistle an' I'll come to ye, my lad!

I

But warily tent when ye come to court me,
And come nae unless the back-yett be a-jee;
Syne up the back-style, and let naebody see,
And come as ye were na comin to me,
And come as ye were na comin to me!

II

At kirk, or at market, whene'er ye meet me,
Gang by me as tho' that ye car'd na a flie;
But steal me a blink o' your bonie black e'e,
Yet look as ye were na lookin to me,
Yet look as ye were na lookin to me!

III

Ay vow and protest that ye care na for me,
And whyles ye may lightly my beauty a wee;
But court na anither tho' jokin ye be,
For fear that she wyle your fancy frae me,
For fear that she wyle your fancy frae me!

CHORUS

O, whistle an' I 'll come to ye, my lad!
O, whistle an' I 'll come to ye, my lad!
Tho' father an' mother an' a' should gae mad,
O, whistle an' I 'll come to ye, my lad!

John Anderson My Jo

I

John Anderson my jo, John,
　　When we were first acquent,
Your locks were like the raven,
　　Your bonie brow was brent;
But now your brow is beld, John,
　　Your locks are like the snaw,
But blessings on your frosty pow,
　　John Anderson my jo!

II

John Anderson my jo, John,
　　We clamb the hill thegither,
And monie a cantie day, John,
　　We 've had wi' ane anither;
Now we maun totter down, John,
　　And hand in hand we 'll go,
And sleep thegither at the foot,
　　John Anderson my jo!

A Red, Red Rose

I

O, my luve is like a red, red rose,
　　That 's newly sprung in June.
O, my luve is like the melodie,
　　That 's sweetly play'd in tune.

II

As fair art thou, my bonie lass,
　　So deep in luve am I,

And I will luve thee still, my dear,
   Till a' the seas gang dry.

III

Till a' the seas gang dry, my dear,
   And the rocks melt wi' the sun!
And I will luve thee still, my dear,
   While the sands o' life shall run.

IV

And fare thee weel, my only luve,
   And fare thee weel a while!
And I will come again, my luve,
   Tho' it were ten thousand mile!

Auld Lang Syne

CHORUS

For auld lang syne, my dear,
   For auld lang syne,
We'll tak a cup o' kindness yet
   For auld lang syne!

I

Should auld acquaintance be forgot,
   And never brought to mind?
Should auld acquaintance be forgot,
   And auld lang syne!

II

And surely ye'll be your pint-stowp,
   And surely I'll be mine,

And we'll tak a cup o' kindness yet
   For auld lang syne!

III

We twa hae run about the braes,
   And pou'd the gowans fine,
But we've wander'd monie a weary fit
   Sin' auld lang syne.

IV

We twa hae paidl'd in the burn
   Frae morning sun till dine,
But seas between us braid hae roar'd
   Sin' auld lang syne.

V

And there's a hand, my trusty fiere,
   And gie's a hand o' thine,
And we'll tak a right guid-willie waught
   For auld lang syne!

CHORUS

For auld lang syne, my dear,
   For auld lang syne,
We'll tak a cup o' kindness yet
   For auld lang syne!

Comin Thro' the Rye

O, Jenny 's a' weet, poor body,
    Jenny 's seldom dry:
She draigl't a' her petticoatie,
    Comin thro' the rye!

I

Comin thro' the rye, poor body,
    Comin thro' the rye,
She draigl't a' her petticoatie,
    Comin thro' the rye!

II

Gin a body meet a body
    Comin thro' the rye,
Gin a body kiss a body,
    Need a body cry?

III

Gin a body meet a body
    Comin thro' the glen,
Gin a body kiss a body,
    Need the warld ken?

CHORUS

O, Jenny 's a' weet, poor body,
    Jenny 's seldom dry:
She draigl't a' her petticoatie,
    Comin thro' the rye!

FROM THOMSON'S *SCOTISH AIRS*

Scots, Wha Hae

I

Scots, wha hae wi' Wallace bled,
Scots, wham Bruce has aften led,
Welcome to your gory bed
                   Or to victorie!

II

Now's the day, and now's the hour:
See the front o' battle lour,
See approach proud Edward's power—
                   Chains and slaverie!

III

Wha will be a traitor knave?
Wha can fill a coward's grave?
Wha sae base as be a slave?—
                   Let him turn, and flee!

IV

Wha for Scotland's King and Law
Freedom's sword will strongly draw,
Freeman stand or freeman fa',
                   Let him follow me!

V

By Oppression's woes and pains,
By your sons in servile chains,
We will drain our dearest veins
                   But they shall be free!

VI

Lay the proud usurpers low!
Tyrants fall in every foe!
Liberty's in every blow!
                   Let us do, or die!

FROM *THE MERRY MUSES OF CALEDONIA*

Brose an' Butter

Gie my Love brose, brose,
   Gie my Love brose an' butter;
An' gie my Love brose, brose,
   Yestreen he wanted his supper.

Jenny sits up i' the laft,
   Jocky wad fain a been at her;
There cam a win' out o' the wast
   Made a' the windows to clatter.

                   Gie my Love brose &c.

A dow's a dainty dish;
   A goose is hollow within;
A sight wad mak you blush,
   But a' the fun's to fin'.

                   Gie my &c.

My Dadie sent me to the hill,
   To pow my minnie some heather;

An' drive it in your fill,
  Ye're welcome to the leather.

            Gie my &c.

A mouse is a merry wee beast;
  A modewurck wants the een;
An' O for the touch o' the thing
  I had i' my nieve yestreen.

            Gie my Love &c.

The lark she loves the grass;
  The hen she loves the stibble;
An' hey for the Gar'ner lad,
  To gully awa wi' his dibble.—

Wha 'll Mow Me Now?

TUNE: *"Comin Thro' the Rye"*

O, I hae tint my rosy cheek,
  Likewise my waste sae sma';
O wae gae by the sodger lown,
  The sodger did it a'.

  O wha 'll m—w me now, my jo,
    An' wha 'll m—w me now:
  A sodger wi' his bandileers
    Has bang'd my belly fu'.

Now I maun thole the scornfu' sneer
  O' mony a saucy quine;

When, curse upon her godly face!
　　Her c—t's as merry 's mine.

Our dame hauds up her wanton tail,
　　As due as she gaes lie;
An' yet misca's [a] young thing,
　　The trade if she but try.

Our dame can lae her ain gudeman,
　　An' m—w for glutton greed;
An' yet misca's a poor thing,
　　That's m—n' for its bread.

Alake! sae sweet a tree as love,
　　Sic bitter fruit should bear!
Alake, that e'er a merry a—e,
　　Should draw a sa'tty tear.

But deevil damn the lousy loon,
　　Denies the bairn he got!
Or lea's the merry a—e he lo'ed,
　　To wear a ragged coat!

Glossary

❖❖

Note: This glossary is derived largely from that provided by Professor James Kinsley in Burns, *Poems and Songs* (Oxford: Oxford University Press, 1971). Words not included here that are difficult to understand may be checked in that source, although one might first consult a standard English dictionary (e.g., "lawn-sleeve").

ae one; used also for emphasis
aff-hand at once, on the spur of the moment
agley wrong
aiblins perhaps
aith oath
aiver old horse
a-jee ajar
asklent askew, askance
aumous dish alms dish
ava of all, at all
ayont beyond

bane bone, bone-comb
bann'd cursed
batts colic
bauckie-bird bat
baudrons cat
beets kindles
belyve quickly
benmost innermost
bestead placed

bicker scurry
bien cosy
big build
billy comrade, fellow, friend
birk birch tree
blate bashful
bleeze blaze
blellum babbler
blink glance fondly, leer
boddle coin struck by Charles I; a sixth of an English penny
bogle ghost
boord surface
boost must
bootree shrub elder in a barnyard hedge
bore crevice, crack
botches boils
bowse; bouze booze, drink heavily; drinking party
branks halter, bridle
brattle hurry
brig bridge
brose oatmeal mixed with boiling water or milk
bumman humming
burdies girls
byke swarm, crowd

cadger peddler
caird gypsy, tinker
calf-ward churchyard
callet wench, trollop
cantraip magic
canty lively, cheerfully
carlin old woman, old fellow
cartes cards

cauk drawing
chapman peddler
claith clothing
clash chatter, gossip
clautet gripped, scraped
cleek pilfer, lay hold of
clish-ma-claver tittle-tattle
cloots cloven-footed
clouted patched
coft bought
coggie drinking vessel; womb
coofs louts
coor protect, cover
coost cast, discarded
cootie basin, tub
cour lower, fold
cowe terrify; terror
cowpit blown over, laid low
cowte colt; awkward person
craigie throat, gullet
cranreuch frost
creeshie greasy, dirty
croose merry, cocky
crowlan creeping
crummock crook
curmurring flatulence
cutty short, brief

dadie daddy, father
daffin flirtation, dallying
daimen-icker occasional ear of corn
daud abuse, pelt
daut; dautet, dawtit fondle, pet; fondled, spoiled

dight make ready; wipe down
ding weary, worn out
dirl rattle; play vigorously
douse sober, prudent; kindly
dow, dought dare to, be able; dared
driddle saunter; totter
droddum backside
drouthy thirsty
dub puddle, pond, mire
duddies clothes; rags

e'e; een eye; eyes
elbuck elbow
eldritch uncanny; haunted; hideous
ell unit of measurement (37.059 inches)
Erse Highland, Gaelic
ettle purpose

fallow fellow
fash bother
fash'd troubled
fatt'rels ribbon ends
fauld (sheep) fold; gather in, pen
fell cuticle
ferlie marvel
fidge shrug, twitch
fier sound, healthy
fit(t) foot
flainen flannel
fodgel plump; good-humored
foggage rank grass
fouth plenty
fud backside, tail
fyke fidget, fuss

geck scoff at
gimmer-pet yearling ewe kept as a pet
gin before; if
girdle griddle
gleg quick, smart
goom gum
gowan weed flower
graith equipment, dress
grozet gooseberry
gullie, gully large knife; cut, dig

haet have it; take it
haffet temple; lock of hair
hainch haunch
hald hold; refuge
harn sackcloth
haud hold
heeze lift, exalt
hilch limp
hing hang
hizzie silly girl; whore
houlet owl
hove rise; cause to swell
howcket dug up
hoyse hoist
hurchin hedgehog; urchin
hurdies buttocks

ilka each, every
ingine talent; wit
ingle fire burning on a hearth

jad mare; hussy
jaup splash

jinkan dodging
jocteleg clasp knife
Johnny Ged's-Hole grave digger

kail kale; semen
kail-runt stalk stripped of leaves
kebar rafter
kintra country
kirn churn; harvest merrymaking
kirs'n christen
kittle rouse; tricky
knappin-hammer hammer for breaking stones
kyte belly

laggen angles between the sides and bottom of a dish
lallan(d) lowland
lave others, rest
laverock lark
lear lore, learning
leister trident
leugh laugh
link skip, go briskly
linkan skipping
lough lake
loun rascal; whore
lowan heugh flaming pit
lowe blaze
lowse loose
luggie wooden dish with staves projecting for handles
Lunardi style of bonnet named after an Italian balloonist
lyart grizzled

mailin small holding; leased land
meikle, muckle much, plentiful

melder quantity of meal ground for a customer at one time
minnie mommy, mother
mislear'd mischievous
moudiewart mole; penis
mow have sexual relations with, fuck
mutchkin quarter-pint (Scots)

nappy ale
niest next
nieve fist
niger black person

orra spare

paetrick partridge; girl
painch paunch, belly
pattle small spade used to clean a plow
paughty proud, arrogant
philibeg kilt
pin skewer; penis
plack coin of small worth
pleugh plow
pliver green plover; peewit
pock bag
poossie puss; derogatory term for a woman
pow head
pownie pony
pyke pick at

quean, quine young girl; jade
quech shallow drinking vessel
queir choir

rash-buss clump of rushes
ratton rat

raucle rough, coarse
rax stretch; elastic
rede advise, warn
reeket smoky, smoked
reestet gizz smoked wig
rigwoodie back-band for a cart-horse; coarse; withered
rive break up, burst
roose praise, boast
rowte bellow, roar
rozet resin
ryke reach

sair sore; sorry, sad
sark shirt, chemise, shift
sa'tty salty
saut-backet small box for salt kept near the kitchen fireplace
scaud scald
scaur afraid
scawl a scold
sconner feel sick; disgust
sel self
shangan stick for teasing or frightening dogs
shavie trick
sheugh ditch
shog shock, jolt
shore threaten; offer
siller silver
skaith hurt, damage
skellum rascal
skelp strike; smack(ing kiss)
skinking watery
sklentan squinting greedily; eyeing obliquely
sklented slanting
skyte sudden blow

slade steal away
slap gap in a fence or dike
slight skill
smeddum powder used as insecticide or medicine
smoored smothered
smoutie phiz ugly face
sned cut off, prune
snell keen, bitter
snick-drawing crafty
snirtle snigger
sodger soldier
sonsie good-natured; buxom
sowth try a tune by whistling it softly
spairge plaster; splatter
spavet spavined
spavie spavin, tumor
spean wean
spier inquire
spier't ask of
spleuchan purse; pudenda
splore frolic, uproar
spunk will-o'-the-wisp; whiskey
spurtle-blade sword
stacher stagger
stane stone
stap stop
staw stole
steek shut
stibble stubble
stirk young bull
stoiter stagger
stoor, stoure harsh, stern; battle; storm
stowp tankard; measure
swither flurry

syne since
synsine since then

tacket hobnail
tap top
Tarry-Breeks nickname for a sailor
tent care for; take heed of
thairms intestines; fiddle strings
thegither together
thole endure, suffer
thrang throng, crowd
thrave measure of straw
thrissle thistle
thy-lane yourself alone
tint lost
tirl rattle at a door
tither the other
toom empty
towmont twelve-month, year
towsing handling roughly
towzie shaggy, unkempt
trepan beguile
trogger peddler
twal twelve
twal-pint giving twelve pints at a milking
tyta daddy, father

unco odd
usquabae, usquebae whiskey

vauntie vain, proud

wae woe
wale choice; choose

walie, wawlie handsome; ample
wame belly; uterus
warklum tool for work; penis
waur worse
wean child
wee little
weet wet; rain
whang thick slice of cheese; flog
whid move quickly and quietly
whin gorse
whitter draft of liquor
whittle clasp knife
whyles now and then, sometimes
winna will not, won't
winnock-bunker window seat
wonner wonder
wordy worthy
wylecoat flannel vest

yett gate
yill ale
yokin contest; coupling

About the Editor

❖

Robert Creeley has published a number of books, among them The Collected Poems, 1945–1975, The Collected Prose, *and* The Collected Essays. *He is Samuel P. Capen Professor of Humanities at the State University of New York at Buffalo.*